DINOSAURS RULED!

ANKYLOSAURUS

LEIGH ROCKWOOD

PowerKiDS
press™
New York

Published in 2012 by The Rosen Publishing Group, Inc.
29 East 21st Street, New York, NY 10010

First Edition

Editor: Joanne Randolph
Book Design: Kate Laczynski

Photo Credits: Cover, title page by Brian Garvey; cover background (palm tree leaves) © www.iStockphoto.com/dra_schwartz; cover background (palm tree trunk), p. 9 iStockphoto/Thinkstock; cover background (ginkgo leaves) Hemera/Thinkstock; cover background (fern leaves) Brand X Pictures/Thinkstock; cover background (moss texture) © www.iStockphoto.com/Robert Linton; pp. 4–5, 6, 7, 8, 10, 11, 13, 14, 15, 16, 19, 20–21 © 2011 Orpheus Books Ltd.; pp. 12, 22 Louie Psihoyos/Getty Images; p. 17 John Foxx/Stockbyte/Thinkstock; p. 18 De Agostini/Getty Images.

Library of Congress Cataloging-in-Publication Data

Rockwood, Leigh.
 Ankylosaurus / by Leigh Rockwood. — 1st ed.
     p. cm. — (Dinosaurs ruled!)
 Includes index.
 ISBN 978-1-4488-4967-3 (library binding) — ISBN 978-1-4488-5084-6 (pbk.) — ISBN 978-1-4488-5085-3 (6-pack)
 1. Ankylosaurus—Juvenile literature. I. Title.
 QE862.O65R623 2012
 567.915—dc22
                                        2010051360

Manufactured in the United States of America

CPSIA Compliance Information: Batch #WS11PK: For Further Information contact Rosen Publishing, New York, New York at 1-800-237-9932

CONTENTS

Meet the Ankylosaurus 4

The Late Cretaceous Period 6

Where Did the Ankylosaurus Live? 8

The Ankylosaurus's Body 10

Armored Dinosaur 12

Tale of the Tail 14

A Plant-Eating Dinosaur 16

Making Tracks 18

Tough Prey 20

No Bones About It 22

GLOSSARY 23

INDEX 24

WEB SITES 24

MEET THE ANKYLOSAURUS

The ankylosaurus was one tough-looking dinosaur! Its body was covered in hard, bony plates that kept it safe from **predators**. This dinosaur also had a clublike tail, which it could use to hit predators that got too close. The ankylosaurus gets its name from its plated body. "Ankylosaurus" means "fused lizard." The ankylosaurus's plates look as though they have been fused to its body. "Fused" means "melted together."

Ankylosaurus **fossils** give **paleontologists** clues about the dinosaur. By studying fossils, scientists have come up with new theories, or ideas, about animals that have been **extinct** for millions of years.

The ankylosaurus was a slow-moving plant eater. It kept itself safe from enemies with its bony skin and its powerful tail.

THE LATE CRETACEOUS PERIOD

DINO BITE

The ankylosaurus lived at the very end of the Late Cretaceous period. Based on the fossils that have been found, paleontologists theorize that the ankylosaurus wa one of the last dinosaurs to become extinct.

Earth's long history is measured using geologic time. The ankylosaurus lived during the Late Cretaceous period, which lasted from about 89 to 65 million years ago.

The ankylosaurus was a plant eater, and many kinds of plants grew in the warm, wet **climate** of the Late Cretaceous period. Plant-eating dinosaurs like the

The ankylosaurus was the biggest of the armored dinosaurs known as ankylosaurids. There were plenty of other dinosaurs that were larger than it, though!

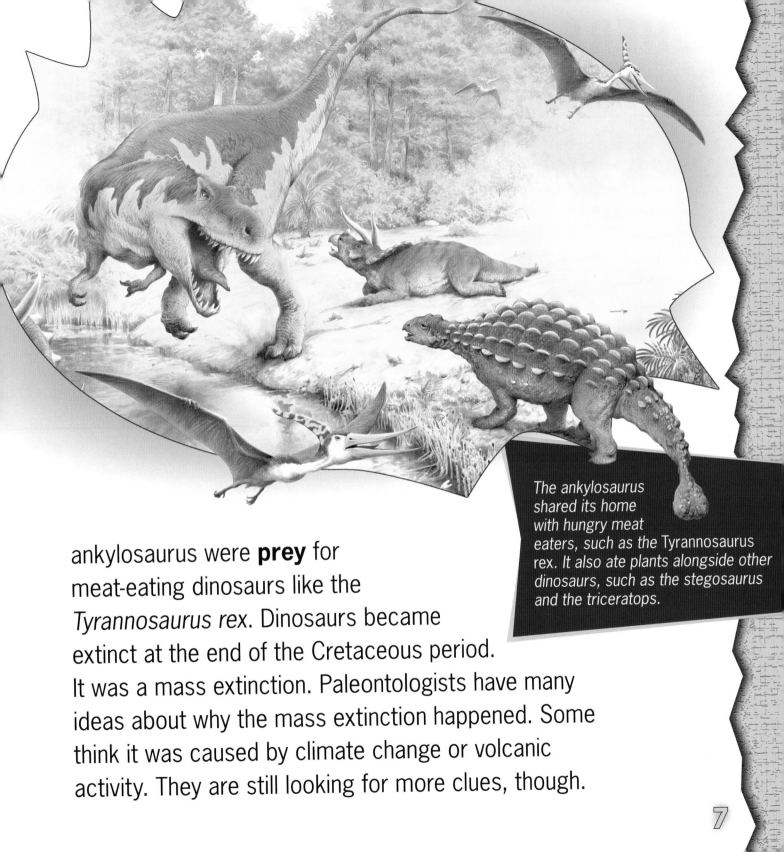

The ankylosaurus shared its home with hungry meat eaters, such as the Tyrannosaurus rex. It also ate plants alongside other dinosaurs, such as the stegosaurus and the triceratops.

ankylosaurus were **prey** for meat-eating dinosaurs like the Tyrannosaurus rex. Dinosaurs became extinct at the end of the Cretaceous period. It was a mass extinction. Paleontologists have many ideas about why the mass extinction happened. Some think it was caused by climate change or volcanic activity. They are still looking for more clues, though.

WHERE DID THE ANKYLOSAURUS LIVE?

The ankylosaurus lived in what is today's northern North America. Ankylosaurus fossils have been found in Montana and in Canada. In the Late Cretaceous period, these lands were warm and full of plant life. Today these places are mostly colder and drier than they were then.

The ankylosaurus lived in warm, wet places where lots of plants grew. This was important to the ankylosaurus since it needed to eat a lot of plants to stay alive!

DINO BITE

Ankylosaurus tracks were found in Bolivia, in South America, in 1996.

The places where the ankylosaurus once lived are full of the **sedimentary rocks** in which fossils are found. These rocks form when sediment is pressed together for millions of years. Sediment is made up of layers of sand, mud, or stone. Fossils form when dead plants or animals become trapped in sediment. Everything that is known about the ankylosaurus so far comes from just two fossilized skulls and three partial fossilized skeletons!

Ankylosaurus fossils have been found in many places, including the Hell Creek rock formation in Montana. Pompey's Pillar, shown here, is part of the Hell Creek formation.

THE ANKYLOSAURUS'S BODY

The overall look of an ankylosaurus's body might make you think of a long, low tank. When fully grown, this dinosaur was about 25 to 35 feet (8–11 m) long and 6 feet (2 m) wide. It stood 4 feet (1 m) tall and weighed 3 to 4 tons (3–4 t).

The ankylosaurus was not very tall, but it was long and wide. Its bony skin was covered in bumps and spikes, too.

Ankylosaurs, such as this relative of the ankylosaurus, had longer back legs than front legs.

The top of the ankylosaurus's body was covered in thick plates that kept its body safe. Its tail ended in a bony growth that the dinosaur could have used to hit its enemies. An ankylosaurus's underside did not have any plates to keep it safe, though. If a predator like the *Tyrannosaurus rex* flipped over an ankylosaurus, it could hurt or kill that dinosaur.

ARMORED DINOSAUR

The ankylosaurus is sometimes called an armored dinosaur because of its thick, bony plates. These bony plates are called **osteoderms**. The ankylosaurus had more than just bony plates, though. Two rows of spikes ran the length of its body. It also had horns on its head. It is thought that the horns did not point out

These are fossilized plates from an ankylosaur. The osteoderms, also called scutes, were different shapes and sizes and covered most of the dinosaur's body.

Here you can see the bony plates and spikes that make up this ankylosaur's body covering. It is using its clublike tail to hit predators. Ankylosaurs were not easy meals.

toward predators. Instead, some paleontologists think the horns pointed up and helped males draw **mates**.

The ankylosaurus had short legs compared to the rest of its body. This made it harder for predators to flip the dinosaur over to get at its soft belly.

TALE OF THE TAIL

Bony plates were not the only things keeping the ankylosaurus safe. It also used its tail to **defend** itself. The vertebrae, or tailbones, of the tail were fused together. At the very end of the tail were more osteoderms like those on its sides and back. The tail was likely very stiff and hard for the dinosaur to move. If an ankylosaur hit an enemy with its tail, though, that unlucky dinosaur likely felt some pain!

The ankylosaurus's tail had extra bones in it that formed a club. The dinosaur could likely swing it only from side to side.

This relative of the ankylosaurus, called a talarurus, is using its tail to fight off a hungry predator.

The ankylosaurus's brain was small compared to the size of its body. Because of this, paleontologists think this dinosaur was not one of the smarter dinosaurs.

A PLANT-EATING DINOSAUR

DINO BITE

An ankylosaurus's teeth were small and suited to chewing leaves. Its teeth looked a lot like those of the stegosaurus, another plant-eating dinosaur.

The ankylosaurus was an **herbivore**. An herbivore is an animal that eats only plants. The ankylosaurus had to eat a large amount of plants to keep its big body going.

The ankylosaurus had a beaklike mouth and small teeth that it used to graze on low-lying plants, grasses, and bushes.

Ankylosaurs had beaklike mouths, just as other plant-eating dinosaurs did.

Paleontologists think that this dinosaur had special organs to help it break down the large amount of plants it ate. Such organs would have made the plants **ferment** in the dinosaur's gut. This means that the ankylosaurus would have passed a lot of gas!

Anylosaurs ate lots of plants that grew low to the ground, such as ferns and grasses. Ferns still grow in forests today.

MAKING TRACKS

In 1996, fossilized ankylosaur tracks were found in Bolivia. Paleontologists studied these tracks to learn more about how the dinosaur moved. First they looked at the distance between the tracks and the pattern in which the dinosaur's feet fell. Then they compared those observations with the length of the legs on an ankylosaurus fossil.

Can you imagine this tanklike dinosaur running toward you? Many predators, faced with the same sight, likely looked elsewhere for food.

Many fossilized ankylosaur tracks were likely left in places that were once near water. From the number of tracks found in each place, scientists think these dinosaurs likely lived alone most of the time.

Studying all of these things gave the scientists an idea of the ankylosaurus's **stride**. An animal's stride is longer when it is running than when it is walking. Based on their observations, scientists theorized that while the ankylosaurus was not a very fast animal, it could run a little bit when it needed to.

TOUGH PREY

In the Late Cretaceous period, there were many large meat-eating dinosaurs. These hungry dinosaurs preyed on plant-eating dinosaurs, such as the ankylosaurus. The most famous predator of this time was the T. rex. Other predators included deinonychus and tarbosaurus.

It is thought that the ankylosaurus was

This predator with the red crest on its head would likely have chosen to hunt the smaller dinosaur guarding its nest instead of the ankylosaur.

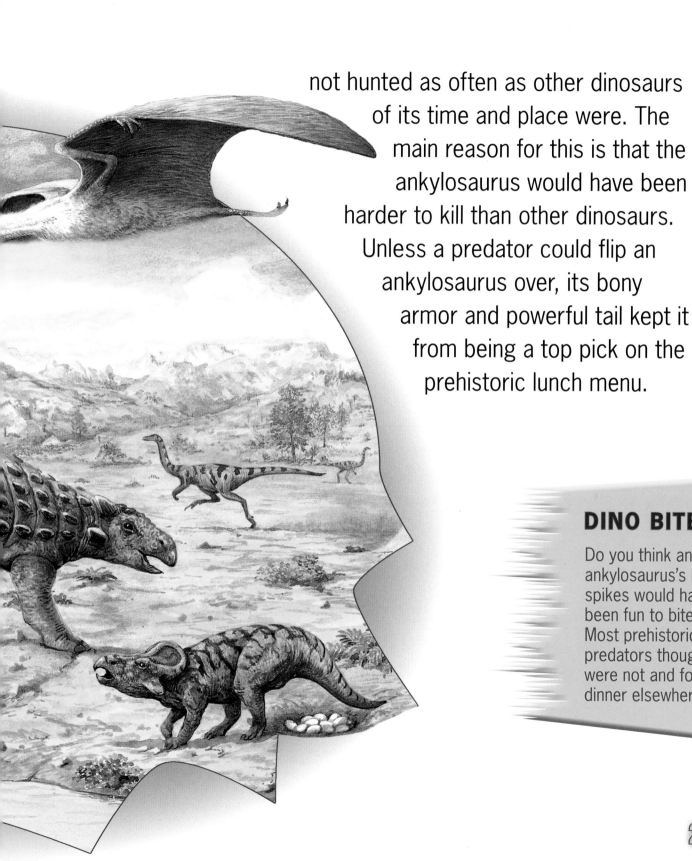

not hunted as often as other dinosaurs of its time and place were. The main reason for this is that the ankylosaurus would have been harder to kill than other dinosaurs. Unless a predator could flip an ankylosaurus over, its bony armor and powerful tail kept it from being a top pick on the prehistoric lunch menu.

DINO BITE

Do you think an ankylosaurus's bony spikes would have been fun to bite? Most prehistoric predators thought they were not and found dinner elsewhere.

NO BONES ABOUT IT

The first ankylosaurus fossils were found in the early 1900s. The paleontologist Barnum Brown gave the ankylosaurus its name in 1908. Very few ankylosaurus fossils have been found. Even so, the two skulls, three partial skeletons, and tracks that have been found have given paleontologists some important clues about this dinosaur.

Here a paleontologist puts together an ankylosaurus skeleton found in the Gobi Desert.

When a fossil is found, paleontologists carefully remove the rocks and dirt around it. With so few fossils, there are many things that are not known about the ankylosaurus. If more fossils are found in the future, paleontologists will have a chance to learn new things or to change existing ideas about this armored dinosaur.

GLOSSARY

climate (KLY-mut) The kind of weather a certain place has.

defend (dih-FEND) To guard from being hurt.

extinct (ik-STINGKT) No longer existing.

ferment (fer-MENT) To change in a way that makes gas bubbles.

fossils (FO-sulz) The hardened remains of dead animals or plants.

herbivore (ER-buh-vor) An animal that eats only plants.

mates (MAYTS) Partners for making babies.

osteoderms (OS-tee-uh-dermz) Bony plates that are part of the skin.

paleontologists (pay-lee-on-TAH-luh-jists) People who study things that lived in the past.

predators (PREH-duh-terz) Animals that kill other animals for food.

prey (PRAY) An animal that is hunted by another animal for food.

sedimentary rocks (seh-deh-MEN-teh-ree ROKS) Stones, sand, or mud that has been pressed together to form rock.

stride (STRYD) The length of one step.

INDEX

B
body, 4, 10–13, 15–16

C
climate, 6

F
fossil(s), 4, 8–9, 18, 22

G
geologic time, 6

H
herbivore, 16
history, 6

I
ideas, 4, 7, 19, 22

M
mates, 13

N
name, 4, 22

O
osteoderms, 12, 14

P
paleontologists, 4, 7, 13, 15, 17–18, 22
plants, 6, 9, 16–17

plates, 4, 11–12, 14
predator(s), 4, 11, 13, 20–21
prey, 7

S
scientists, 4, 19
sedimentary rocks, 9
stride, 19

T
tail, 4, 11, 14, 21
theories, 4
Tyrannosaurus rex, 7, 11, 20

WEB SITES

Due to the changing nature of Internet links, PowerKids Press has developed an online list of Web sites related to the subject of this book. This site is updated regularly. Please use this link to access the list:
www.powerkidslinks.com/dinr/anklo/